Instant Hands-on Testing with PHPUnit How-to

A practical guide to getting started with PHPUnit to improve code quality

Michael Lively

BIRMINGHAM - MUMBAI

Instant Hands-on Testing with PHPUnit How-to

First published: May 2013

Production Reference: 1170513

Published by Packt Publishing Ltd.
Livery Place
35 Livery Street
Birmingham B3 2PB, UK.

ISBN 978-1-78216-958-1

www.packtpub.com

Credits

Author
Michael Lively

Reviewers
Brian Feaver

Adam Englander

Acquisition Editor
Mary Jasmine Nadar

Commissioning Editor
Yogesh Dalvi

Technical Editor
Worrell Lewis

Project Coordinator
Michelle Quadros

Proofreader
Lydia May Morris

Production Coordinator
Melwyn D'sa

Cover Work
Melwyn D'sa

Cover Image
Aditi Gajjar

About the Author

Michael Lively has worked in a variety of roles in the software development industry for 12 years, from developer to architect and now a software development director. He has worked on a variety of different projects and a variety of different technologies over that time, from small home-grown sites serving a handful of regular users to large enterprise platforms serving millions of consumers. In addition to his professional work, he has been an active member of the PHP open source community. Some of his contributions include the database extension for PHPUnit and more recently an alternative mocking framework for PHP called Phake.

I would like to thank everyone who, over the years, has given me opportunities to work in and with the technology industry. From my schooling to the present day I have had the fortunate blessing of meeting some of the most gifted and knowledgeable folks in the IT industry. Specifically, I would like to thank Sebastian Bergmann who introduced me to unit testing and provided me great opportunities to contribute back to the community. I would also like to thank Brian Feaver and Adam Englander. Both are fantastic co-workers and gave me lots of great feedback when I discussed topics for this book with them.

Last but certainly not least this journey called life would not be nearly as complete without my girls. I would like to thank my wonderful wife Sharon and my fantastic girls Trinity, Hannah, and Gracelyn. Their patience and willingness to chase my goals with me has made all the difference in the world.

About the Reviewers

Brian Feaver is the Lead Software Architect at Selling Source LLC. He's been a software developer for over 10 years, contributes to multiple open source projects, and participates in developer-user communities. He is a strong advocate of developer testing and automated testing in general.

Adam Englander is the CTO of Coupla where he leads their development and cloud platform initiatives. He is an accomplished software professional with more than 25 years of architecting and developing critical business systems. He is a testing evangelist and resource to the development community. He develops testing tools and, in addition, speaks to various groups about these tools and the testing methodologies in general.

Coupla is an online community with the singular goal of making stronger couples relationships. Coupla is a proud member of Vegas Tech and the Las Vegas Startup Community.

www.PacktPub.com

Support files, eBooks, discount offers and more

You might want to visit www.PacktPub.com for support files and downloads related to your book.

Did you know that Packt offers eBook versions of every book published, with PDF and ePub files available? You can upgrade to the eBook version at www.PacktPub.com and as a print book customer, you are entitled to a discount on the eBook copy. Get in touch with us at service@packtpub.com for more details.

At www.PacktPub.com, you can also read a collection of free technical articles, sign up for a range of free newsletters and receive exclusive discounts and offers on Packt books and eBooks.

http://PacktLib.PacktPub.com

Do you need instant solutions to your IT questions? PacktLib is Packt's online digital book library. Here, you can access, read and search across Packt's entire library of books.

Why Subscribe?

- ▸ Fully searchable across every book published by Packt
- ▸ Copy and paste, print and bookmark content
- ▸ On demand and accessible via web browser

Free Access for Packt account holders

If you have an account with Packt at www.PacktPub.com, you can use this to access PacktLib today and view nine entirely free books. Simply use your login credentials for immediate access.

Table of Contents

Preface

The goal of almost every software developer is to create code that is free from defects and works as intended. To help ensure this goal is met we spend a significant amount of time testing the code that we have written. As software grows in size and complexity the likelihood of defects being introduced increases. Naturally, we have to increase our efforts in testing to help accommodate the increased risk.

When I first began writing software I would test my applications by manually running through a series of steps on a deployed application. I would add items to my cart, I would remove them again, I would manually check to make sure taxes and shipping costs were calculated correctly. I spent a lot of time looking at as much functionality as I could think of. Commonly, I would miss some less obvious pieces of functionality and small bugs would slowly creep into the code as the software aged and my memory of the intricate details of how it worked faded.

Fortunately, I was introduced to the concept of automated testing fairly early on in my career. Automated testing, specifically automated unit testing is a powerful tool in any programmer's arsenal. It allows us to have an easily repeatable way to check and make sure the software we write is working the way we intend. It provides future maintainers of the code with the ability to have confidence that they can change functionality and not be worried that they will regress the code back to old errors. It gives us freedom as software developers to focus more time on moving our software forward instead of living in fear that any change we make will cause the system to break.

There are many tools to help you write effective unit tests quickly. In PHP, the leading tool is PHPUnit. In this book, we are going to learn how you can use PHPUnit in your project to create a test suite that can give you an increased level of confidence in the software you are writing.

What this book covers

Installing PHPUnit (Simple) will teach you how to install PHPUnit using the PEAR package manager. You will also learn about some alternative ways to install PHPUnit.

Writing your first test (Simple) will help you create a basic test and learn about the common phases of a unit test written in PHPUnit.

Running tests (Simple) will show you how to run your tests using the command line tool and gain some insight into the various options the tool gives you.

Configuring PHPUnit (Simple) will show you how to move the configuration of PHPUnit from the command line to configuration files that can easily be shared as a part of your project.

Adding PHPUnit to your project (Simple) will teach you the steps necessary to integrate unit tests into your project.

Generating tests from code (Advanced) will show you how the PHPUnit's Skeleton Generator can be utilized to generate tests from existing code. You will even see how you can generate code stubs from tests for true test-driven development.

Using test fixtures (Simple) will teach you how to use shared fixtures to reduce code duplication and to reduce the code necessary to set up new tests.

Using data providers (Intermediate) will show you how data providers can be leveraged to rapidly create test cases that validate a variety of calls using separate data points.

Using test dependencies (Advanced) will show you how you can isolate failed tests by using a consumer-producer pattern inside your test cases. This will allow you to spend less time determining which piece of functionality caused your test to fail.

Using mock objects (Simple) will teach you how to leverage mock objects to keep the unit of code being tested small.

Testing abstract classes (Intermediate) will show you how PHPUnit's mock functionality can be used to test abstract classes.

Testing traits (Intermediate) will teach you how you can use PHPUnit to test traits in a very simple yet dynamic way.

Testing exceptions and errors (Intermediate) will show you how you can ensure that the proper errors and exceptions are being thrown from code at the correct time. It is just as important to know that your application fails properly as it is to know it works properly.

Testing output (Intermediate) will teach you how you can leverage PHPUnit's output buffering features to ensure your code is outputting text correctly to your end users.

Testing protected and private methods (Intermediate) will teach you a sound strategy for testing private and protected methods.

Testing database interaction (Advanced) will show you how PHPUnit can be used to ensure your application is working properly with your database.

Viewing code coverage (Advanced) will teach you how PHPUnit's code coverage reporting can give you clues on where both the well tested and the not-so-well tested code resides in your system.

What you need for this book

The examples in this book were written using PHP 5.3.24 and PHPUnit 3.7. All code samples were verified against a Linux box with Ubuntu 12.04 LTS.

Who this book is for

This book is written for anyone who has an interest in unit testing but doesn't necessarily know where to start in integrating it with their project. It will provide useful tips and insights into how PHPUnit can be used with your projects and it should give you enough information to whet your appetite for the various features offered by PHPUnit.

Conventions

In this book, you will find a number of styles of text that distinguish between different kinds of information. Here are some examples of these styles, and an explanation of their meaning.

Code words in text are shown as follows: "The `auto_discover` setting tells PEAR that any time a package from a new channel is requested, it should automatically register that channel."

A block of code is set as follows:

```
{
    "require-dev": {
        "phpunit/phpunit": "3.7.*"
    }
}
```

When we wish to draw your attention to a particular part of a code block, the relevant lines or items are set in bold:

```
<php>
  <includePath>src</includePath>
<const name="DB_DSN" value="sqlite:data/game-test.db" />

</php>
```

Any command-line input or output is written as follows:

```
sudo pear config-set auto_discover 1
sudo pear install pear.phpunit.de/PHPUnit
```

New terms and **important words** are shown in bold. Words that you see on the screen, in menus or dialog boxes for example, appear in the text like this: "clicking the **Next** button moves you to the next screen."

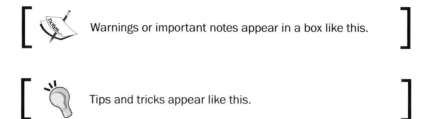

Warnings or important notes appear in a box like this.

Tips and tricks appear like this.

Reader feedback

Feedback from our readers is always welcome. Let us know what you think about this book—what you liked or may have disliked. Reader feedback is important for us to develop titles that you really get the most out of.

To send us general feedback, simply send an e-mail to feedback@packtpub.com, and mention the book title via the subject of your message.

If there is a topic that you have expertise in and you are interested in either writing or contributing to a book, see our author guide on www.packtpub.com/authors.

Customer support

Now that you are the proud owner of a Packt book, we have a number of things to help you to get the most from your purchase.

Downloading the example code

You can download the example code files for all Packt books you have purchased from your account at http://www.packtpub.com. If you purchased this book elsewhere, you can visit http://www.packtpub.com/support and register to have the files e-mailed directly to you.

Errata

Although we have taken every care to ensure the accuracy of our content, mistakes do happen. If you find a mistake in one of our books—maybe a mistake in the text or the code—we would be grateful if you would report this to us. By doing so, you can save other readers from frustration and help us improve subsequent versions of this book. If you find any errata, please report them by visiting http://www.packtpub.com/submit-errata, selecting your book, clicking on the **errata submission form** link, and entering the details of your errata. Once your errata are verified, your submission will be accepted and the errata will be uploaded on our website, or added to any list of existing errata, under the Errata section of that title. Any existing errata can be viewed by selecting your title from http://www.packtpub.com/support.

Piracy

Piracy of copyright material on the Internet is an ongoing problem across all media. At Packt, we take the protection of our copyright and licenses very seriously. If you come across any illegal copies of our works, in any form, on the Internet, please provide us with the location address or website name immediately so that we can pursue a remedy.

Please contact us at copyright@packtpub.com with a link to the suspected pirated material.

We appreciate your help in protecting our authors, and our ability to bring you valuable content.

Questions

You can contact us at questions@packtpub.com if you are having a problem with any aspect of the book, and we will do our best to address it.

Instant Hands-on Testing with PHPUnit How-to

Welcome to *Instant Hands-on Testing with PHPUnit How-to*. PHPUnit is one of the most widely used unit testing frameworks for PHP. It gives developers all the tools necessary to write easy-to-maintain tests. It also gives developers the ability to easily run those tests. This book will give you the knowledge necessary to use these tools in your PHP projects.

We will be going through the process of installing PHPUnit, writing some simple tests, integrating it with a new project, as well as looking into some of the more advanced functionality that PHPUnit is capable of.

Installing PHPUnit (Simple)

The first step to understanding how to test with PHPUnit is to understand how to make it available in our environment. In this recipe, we will install PHPUnit using the **PHP Extension and Application Repository** (**PEAR**) package manager. While PEAR has been available to PHP developers for some time, new packaging frameworks such as Composer have become increasingly more common. We will also cover these additional packaging methods.

How to do it...

Execute the following commands in a shell:

```
sudo pear config-set auto_discover 1
sudo pear install pear.phpunit.de/PHPUnit
```

How it works...

Installing via PEAR will give you access to PHPUnit across all projects in your environment. PHPUnit uses its own PEAR server for distribution. These are called channels. By default, PEAR is only aware of its own channel. The `auto_discover` setting tells PEAR that any time a package from a new channel is requested, it should automatically register that channel. Otherwise, each new channel would have to be added explicitly using `pear channel-discover`. Not only does PHPUnit itself have its own channel, but some of its dependencies are on other custom channels. This is why we use `pear config-set` to enable `auto_discover`. Because we are using `auto_discover`, we only need to run `pear install` to complete the installation.

There's more...

The standard PEAR installation of PHPUnit should provide everything you need to start writing tests. PEAR is a convenient way to install PHPUnit at the environment level. You may find that installing PHPUnit using a dependency manager called Composer works better for your needs.

Installing PHPUnit using Composer

It is becoming more and more common in the PHP world to bundle everything that you need to run and develop an application at the application level. Composer is a dependency manager for PHP that works well in handling this concept. To understand how Composer works and how you can integrate it into your project, read the Getting Started guide on their website at `http://getcomposer.org`. Once you have Composer integrated into your site, you can add the following package to your `composer.json` file:

```
{
    "require-dev": {
        "phpunit/phpunit": "3.7.*"
    }
}
```

This will set up PHPUnit as a development requirement for your package. This works well as you typically don't need your end users to run your tests. Also, you should always double check the PHPUnit page on packagist `https://packagist.org/packages/phpunit/phpunit` to see what the latest version is. Please note that the remaining examples in this book make use of the PEAR installed version of PHPUnit.

Installing PHPUnit on older versions of PHP

Currently, the latest version of PHPUnit is 3.7. This version requires PHP 5.3.3 or higher. If you find yourself using an older version of PHPUnit, due to a bug in PEAR you may have an issue attempting to install PHPUnit.

```
Duplicate package channel://pear.phpunit.de/File_Iterator-1.3.3 found
Duplicate package channel://pear.phpunit.de/File_Iterator-1.3.2 found
install failed
```

If you see these errors then you need to explicitly tell PEAR to install these packages in addition to the PHPUnit package. If you see this error with `File_Iterator`, you will likely see the same error with `Text_Template` as well.

```
sudo pear install pear.phpunit.de/File_Iterator pear.phpunit.de/Text_
Template pear.phpunit.de/PHPUnit
```

This will provide PEAR the information that it needs to be able to install all of the appropriate packages. If you are using a newer version of PHP (5.3.3 or higher) you shouldn't have this problem.

Writing your first test (Simple)

One of the primary goals of PHPUnit is to make it easy to write tests. The easier it is to write tests, the more likely it is that tests will be written. In this recipe, we will discuss the basic parts of a test and how to implement each of those parts in PHPUnit.

Getting ready...

Each test in our system will consist of four parts: the fixture, the test, the verification, and the tear down. The **fixture** sets up the unit that you are testing to have the necessary state for the rest of the test. The **test** then exercises the system, typically by calling a single method. When verifying the test you are just checking to see if the results of our method are what you expected them to be. The **tear down** step is actually very rarely needed in PHP as memory management is handled for you. Occasionally, you may need to close files, delete data, or manage other external resources. The tear down part of a test is the appropriate place to do this work.

How to do it...

We will begin by testing the `Card` class unit.

1. The following code defines that class and should be put in `Card.php`:

```php
<?php
class Card
{
  private $number;
  private $suit;
  public function __construct($number, $suit)
  {
    $this->number = $number;
```

```
      $this->suit = $suit;
    }
    public function getNumber()
    {
      return $this->number;
    }
    public function getSuit()
    {
      return $this->suit;
    }
    public function isInMatchingSet(Card $card)
    {
      return ($this->getNumber() == $card->getNumber());
    }
  }
```

2. The following code defines a test for this unit and should be put in `CardTest.php`:

```php
<?php
require 'Card.php';
class CardTest extends PHPUnit_Framework_TestCase
{
  public function testGetNumber()
  {
    $card = new Card('4', 'spades');
    $actualNumber = $card->getNumber();
    $this->assertEquals(4, $actualNumber, 'Number should be <4>');
  }
  public function testGetSuit()
  {
    $card = new Card('4', 'spades');
    $actualSuit = $card->getSuit();
    $this->assertEquals('spades', $actualSuit, 'Suit should be
<spades>');
  }
  public function testIsInMatchingSet()
  {
    $card = new Card('4', 'spades');
    $matchingCard = new Card('4', 'hearts');
    $this->assertTrue($card->isInMatchingSet($matchingCard),
        '<4 of Spades> should match <4 of Hearts>');
  }
  public function testIsNotInMatchingSet()
  {
    $card = new Card('4', 'spades');
```

```
                $matchingCard = new Card('5', 'hearts');
                $this->assertFalse($card->isInMatchingSet($matchingCard),
                    '<4 of Spades> should not match <5 of Hearts>');
        }
    }
```

How it works...

The `CardTest` class extends the `PHPUnit_Framework_TestCase` class to create our first unit test. The `PHPUnit_Framework_TestCase` class is what makes this a test. It takes care of all of the low-level tasks of testing for us so that we can just focus on writing the tests in an easy and concise manner.

In each of our tests you can see that we first create our fixture: one or more instances of our `Card` classes. Next, we call the method that we are testing. Finally, we utilize PHPUnit's assert methods to verify the results of the tested methods.

We always pass a message as the final argument to our assert functions. This will be displayed by PHPUnit should any of our tests fail due to these assertions. It can be very important as your test suite gets larger and as time passes to have a good description of our failures so that we clearly understand the expected behavior and what broke. Not only will this provide us a reminder of how the test works, it could also be invaluable to anyone else that works on our code in the future.

The other important thing to note is the `require "Card.php"` line. Your test will already have access to any PHPUnit framework classes and functions; however, you must include the code you are testing yourself. If this line is not present, when the test is run you will get an error because PHPUnit doesn't know about the `Card` class. In a later recipe we will see a much easier way to include the code.

There's more...

Even though these are all simple tests, we are beginning to see some of the simplicity of PHPUnit. One of the most important things that we need to know to effectively use PHPUnit is the basic assert methods it supplies. The ability to perform basic value checking is available, but there are also more complicated assertions possible on arrays, objects, and even XML. Have a look at http://www.phpunit.de/manual/current/en/writing-tests-for-phpunit.html#writing-tests-for-phpunit.assertions to see all of the assertion methods you have access to.

Class names

It is a common practice in PHPUnit to name your test case class after the class it is responsible for testing. We are using that method here. The CardTest class is testing the Card class. Naming your test case classes in this fashion makes your tests easier to find and also makes it easier to understand what class a test case is responsible for covering.

Running tests (Simple)

Now that we know how to write tests it is time to learn how to run them. We will run our tests using the phpunit script. It provides very easy to understand output that shows you whether or not your tests have passed or failed. It also provides a wealth of very useful command line options. We will go over the essential options in this recipe.

How to do it...

1. Execute the following command from your test project:

    ```
    $ phpunit CardTest.php
    ```

2. You should see the following result:

```
● ○ ○   environment — vagrant@precise64: /book — ssh — 80×11
vagrant@precise64:/book$ phpunit CardTest.php
PHPUnit 3.7.10 by Sebastian Bergmann.

Configuration read from /book/phpunit.xml.dist

....

Time: 0 seconds, Memory: 4.00Mb

OK (4 tests, 4 assertions)
vagrant@precise64:/book$
```

How it works...

The simplest form of PHPUnit is to pass the filename of the test you want to run as the only parameter. This will cause PHPUnit to load its framework, then it will load your test and execute each method in the test case you specified.

There's more...

You can also pass a directory to the `phpunit` script. If you do this, PHPUnit will scan that directory, along with any child directories. Any file with a name in the `*Test.php` format will then be scanned. Any class found in that file that extends `PHPUnit_Framework_TestCase` will be executed as a test. So if we had, instead, run the following command we would see the exact same output:

```
$ phpunit .
```

This command would find the `CardTest.php` file. After scanning that file it would find the `CardTest` class and proceed to execute it as a test case.

This functionality, in addition to an intelligent directory structure for your code and tests, can yield a very easy way for you to run small groups of tests at a time. This is something that can be helpful when making small, localized changes to a large code base.

Command line options

The previous example is a very simple. However, there are several command line options that you can use to produce more details about the tests, modify the output of the test, or to specify exactly which tests to run. If you run `phpunit -h`, you will see a list of the available options. While you should spend some time looking at all of these options, you can begin by learning how to use those shown as follows:.

--colors

This option makes it obvious very quickly via a color bar whether or not your tests passed or failed. An example of what this looks like can be seen in the following screenshot:

```
● ○ ○   environment — vagrant@precise64: /book — ssh — 80×11
vagrant@precise64:/book$ phpunit --colors CardTest.php
PHPUnit 3.7.10 by Sebastian Bergmann.

Configuration read from /book/phpunit.xml.dist

....

Time: 0 seconds, Memory: 4.00Mb

OK (4 tests, 4 assertions)
vagrant@precise64:/book$
```

--stop-on-error and --stop-on-failure

These options will halt the test execution if one of your tests fails or has an error. If you have a large test suite and you don't want to run through the full suite when a test fails, these options can be very helpful.

--debug

This will print the name of each test as it is being run. This can be very useful if there are severe issues causing PHPUnit to crash.

--strict

This will enable some additional checks to make sure you don't have any potential issues with your tests. For instance, it will report an error if you have defined a test case with no tests, or if a test outputs any text.

Configuring PHPUnit (Simple)

PHPUnit has a variety of command line options. Once we have identified a set of command line options that work well, we will quickly get tired of typing them into a command line. Thankfully, PHPUnit offers an XML configuration file.

This configuration file provides the ability to set any of the command line options. It can also be used to set up various aspects of your test environment such as defining variables, setting the include path, setting other PHP configuration options, and more.

How to do it...

1. The following XML code should be placed in `phpunit.xml`:

```xml
<phpunit
    colors="true"
    strict="true"
    verbose="true"
>
  <testsuites>
    <testsuite name="Go Fish Test Suite">
      <file>CardTest.php</file>
    </testsuite>
  </testsuites>
</phpunit>
```

2. Then we can run the following command:

```
$ phpunit
```

3. We will see that our test case has been run in the colors mode.

How it works...

We are no longer telling the `phpunit` script which test case to run. When we utilize a configuration file we are able to use that file to modify the behavior of PHPUnit. This allows us to get rid of the command line options.

When the `phpunit` script runs, it will look for a file in the current directory called `phpunit.xml`. If this file exists, it will be loaded as a configuration file. You can explicitly specify the configuration file using the following command:

phpunit -c phpunit.xml

In our test file we have enabled the colors, strict, and verbose flags. These are all attributes of the root `<phpunit>` element. Using the `<testsuites>` element we also define which test cases will be run.

The `<testsuites>` element will contain one or more `<testsuite>` elements. The `<testsuite>` element should always have a `name` attribute that gives a short description of the test suite. The `<testsuite>` element will finally contain one or more `<file>` or `<directory>` elements, which define files and directories containing test cases that should be run. You can also specify any number of `<exclude>` elements that will contain a path that will be ignored when searching for test cases.

There's more...

In our example we are using a single `<file>` element to load our `CardTest.php` file. We could just as easily use `<directory>`. The following `<testsuite>` element highlights the difference:

```
<testsuite name="Go Fish Test Suite">
  <directory>.</directory>
</testsuite>
```

When specifying directories it should be kept in mind that by default, only files in that directory and any child directories with the pattern `*Test.php` will be loaded. You can change this behavior using the `suffix` attribute of the `<directory>` element. So we could also use the following configuration to specify this explicitly:

```
<testsuite name="Go Fish Test Suite">
  <directory suffix="Test.php">.</directory>
</testsuite>
```

Additional configurations

There are many other configuration options available in PHPUnit. Some of them we will cover in later recipes. If you would like to explore all of the options you have at your disposal you should view the PHPUnit documentation: `http://www.phpunit.de/manual/current/en/appendixes.configuration.html`.

Using phpunit.xml.dist

As you continue building a test suite you may find yourself using the `phpunit.xml` file to handle environment configurations or other types of configurations that may not always be necessary for some developers. Instead of providing a `phpunit.xml` file, you can provide a `phpunit.xml.dist` file. PHPUnit will attempt to use this file if a `phpunit.xml` file is not found in the current directory. This allows you to package a default configuration in `phpunit.xml.dist` while letting people easily override it by providing their own `phpunit.xml` file.

Adding PHPUnit to your project (Simple)

So far we have worked through some very simple examples involving just a single file that we are testing. In reality, most projects include many different classes and should include many different tests. One of the keys to a successful test strategy for any project is organization of these classes and tests.

Getting ready...

A common strategy for test organizations is separating tests from source code using the directory structure of the projects. A very easy way to do this is by placing a `src` and `test` directory at the root of your project. The `src` directory would contain all of the code required to run your program. Then the `test` directory can contain code that is required to test your program. Within these two directories you can have nearly identical file layouts with the sole exception being the `Test` suffix on the test case class and the `Test.php` suffix on the file.

We will now go through an example of how this type of structure can be set up and utilized in your project.

How to do it...

1. In your project, move your files into the following structure:

```
● ○ ○   environment — vagrant@precise64: /book — ssh — 80×10
vagrant@precise64:/book$ tree
.
|-- phpunit.xml
|-- src
|   `-- Card.php
`-- test
    `-- CardTest.php

2 directories, 3 files
vagrant@precise64:/book$ ▊ ,
```

2. Then, create a `test-bootstrap.php` file with the following content:

```php
<?php

spl_autoload_register(function ($className) {
  $classPath = str_replace(
    array('_', '\\'),
    DIRECTORY_SEPARATOR,
    $className
  ) . '.php';
  require $classPath;
});
```

3. Next, modify your `phpunit.xml` file to contain the following code:

```xml
<phpunit
    bootstrap="test-bootstrap.php"
    colors="false"
    strict="true"
    verbose="true"
>
  <testsuites>
    <testsuite name="Go Fish Test Suite">
      <directory suffix="Test.php">test</directory>
    </testsuite>
  </testsuites>
  <php>
    <includePath>src</includePath>
  </php>
</phpunit>
```

4. Finally, remove the `require` statement that is in `test/CardTest.php`.

How it works...

Here we are introduced to another feature in PHPUnit: the bootstrap file. The bootstrap file is run by `phpunit` prior to running any tests. This makes it a very convenient place to set up our environment as a whole for testability. This could be anything from setting configurations to setting up an autoloader. We have used it for the latter.

In our `test-bootstrap.php` file we have added a call to `spl_autoload_register()` to look for any files in our `include_path` where the path is the same as the class name after all underscores and namespace separators are replaced with a `DIRECTORY_SEPARATOR` constant and the `.php` file extension is added. This is a subset of the PSR-0 standard: `https://github.com/php-fig/fig-standards/blob/master/accepted/PSR-0.md`.

Once our bootstrap file is created we must make PHPUnit aware of the file. To do this you can use the `bootstrap` attribute of the `<phpunit>` element. We also need to set the include path. You can see we have done that using the `<php>` and `<includePath>` elements.

With all of this set up, we can now remove the `require` statements from our test and everything will continue to run normally.

This helps us further meet the goal of making it easy to write tests. We no longer have to maintain file dependencies ourselves. It is all handled for us by virtue of our autoloader and bootstrap. So adding a test is really just a simple matter of creating the test case.

There's more...

Some parts of this recipe should not necessarily be followed verbatim. For instance, there is really little reason to roll your own autoloader. You, most likely, already have an autoloader defined for your project. If you don't have one defined there are several libraries already built that all handle the PSR-0 standard. One such library is the Symfony2 ClassLoader Component: `http://symfony.com/doc/current/components/class_loader.html`. If you are using Composer then you can also take advantage of its autoloader: `http://getcomposer.org/doc/01-basic-usage.md#autoloading`.

Generating tests from code (Advanced)

When you are writing tests for untested legacy code or you do not employ a test-driven development methodology you will frequently find yourself needing to create test cases for already existing classes. PHPUnit has built-in capability to create skeletons for existing classes. This functionality can help you build up your test suite very quickly.

Using this functionality to test legacy code can be very effective. It will create several tests that are marked as incomplete which can be used to help you determine how far away you are from having coverage in all of your class methods.

Getting ready

The skeleton functionality is an add-on that must be installed to PHPUnit. It can be installed via PEAR using the `phpunit/PHPUnit_SkeletonGenerator` package.

```
environment — vagrant@precise64: ~/Book/FullExample — ssh — 100×22
vagrant@precise64:~/Book/FullExample$ sudo pear install phpunit/PHPUnit_SkeletonGenerator
Attempting to discover channel "components.ez.no"...
downloading channel.xml ...
Starting to download channel.xml (591 bytes)
....done: 591 bytes
Auto-discovered channel "components.ez.no", alias "ezc", adding to registry
downloading PHPUnit_SkeletonGenerator-1.2.0.tgz ...
Starting to download PHPUnit_SkeletonGenerator-1.2.0.tgz (11,210 bytes)
...done: 11,210 bytes
downloading ConsoleTools-1.6.1.tgz ...
Starting to download ConsoleTools-1.6.1.tgz (869,994 bytes)
...done: 869,994 bytes
downloading Base-1.8.tgz ...
Starting to download Base-1.8.tgz (236,357 bytes)
...done: 236,357 bytes
install ok: channel://components.ez.no/Base-1.8
install ok: channel://components.ez.no/ConsoleTools-1.6.1
install ok: channel://pear.phpunit.de/PHPUnit_SkeletonGenerator-1.2.0
vagrant@precise64:~/Book/FullExample$
```

In order for the preceding command to work you do need to make sure the `auto_discover` configuration is set to `1`. If you get errors about unrecognized channels you can enable `auto_discover` with the `sudo pear config-set auto_discover 1` command.

If you are using Composer in your project, it is worth noting that there is not a composer package for the Skeleton Generator. You will have to install it manually.

How to do it...

1. Run `phpunit-skelgen --test -- Player src/Player.php PlayerTest test/PlayerTest.php` in the project folder.

2. Open the `test/PlayerTest.php` file. You will see the following code in that file:

```php
<?php
/**
 * Generated by PHPUnit_SkeletonGenerator 1.2.0 on 2013-01-01 at
23:02:55.
 */
class PlayerTest extends PHPUnit_Framework_TestCase
{
    /**
     * @var Player
```

```
    */
    protected $object;

    /**
     * Sets up the fixture, for example, opens a network
connection.
     * This method is called before a test is executed.
     */
    protected function setUp()
    {
        $this->object = new Player;
    }

    /**
     * Tears down the fixture, for example, closes a network
connection.
     * This method is called after a test is executed.
     */
    protected function tearDown()
    {
    }

    /**
     * @covers Player::getName
     * @todo    Implement testGetName().
     */
    public function testGetName()
    {
        // Remove the following lines when you implement this
test.
        $this->markTestIncomplete(
          'This test has not been implemented yet.'
        );
    }

    /**
     * @covers Player::drawCard
     * @todo    Implement testDrawCard().
     */
    public function testDrawCard()
    {
        // Remove the following lines when you implement this
test.
        $this->markTestIncomplete(
          'This test has not been implemented yet.'
```

```
        );
    }
    //...Rest of tests
}
```

How it works...

The `phpunit-skelgen` command takes up to four parameters. The format of the command is `phpunit-skelgen --test -- <Class Name> <Class File Path> <Test Class Name> <Test Class File Path>`. The class names should be fully qualified class names including the namespace. There are variants of this command that you can use that will look for the file based on the name; however, being as explicit with this command as possible will give you better, more predictable results.

One thing that you will notice is that the skeleton does not properly invoke your constructor. You have to handle this piece of the test case manually. Once that is done you will see that all of the tests return **Incomplete** as the status. As you fill out the tests they will change from incomplete tests to passing tests.

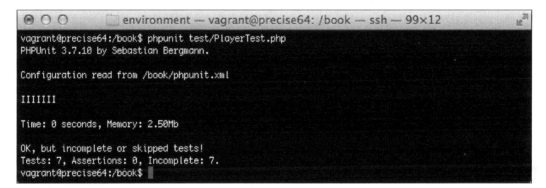

There's more...

The PHPUnit Skeleton Generator is a very powerful command. So far we have barely scratched the surface of how you can use it. When you combine it with PHPDoc annotations you can generate some of the actual test code as opposed to incomplete stubs. You can also use the PHPUnit Skeleton Generator to assist in test-driven development.

Using @assert to generate additional code

You can give the generator hints as to what test code should be created using the `@assert` annotation. These annotations should be added directly to the code that you will be testing. The format of the annotation is `@assert (arg1, arg2, …, argn) operation result`. The operation can be any logical comparison such as `==`, `!=`, `<`, or `>` as well as the `throws` string. The logical comparisons are obvious in their use. The `==` operation is the equivalent to the PHPUnit `assertEquals()` method. The `throws` operator is equivalent to the `@expectedException` annotation.

You can see this in action by adding the following comment to the `isInMatchingSet()` method in `src/Card.php`:

```
/**
 * Returns true if the given card is in the same set
 * @param Card $card
 * @return bool
 * @assert (new Card(3, 'h'), new Card(3, 's')) == true
 * @assert (new Card(4, 'h'), new Card(3, 's')) == false
 */
public function isInMatchingSet(Card $card)
```

When you run the `phpunit-skelgen --test -- Card src/Card.php CardTest2 test/CardTest2.php` command and look at the generated `test/CardTest2.php` file you will now see the following test method:

```
/**
 * Generated from @assert (new Card(3, 'h'), new Card(3, 's')) ==
true.
 *
 * @covers Card::isInMatchingSet
 */
public function testIsInMatchingSet()
{
    $this->assertTrue(
        $this->object->isInMatchingSet(new Card(3, 'h'), new Card(3,
's'))
        );
}

/**
 * Generated from @assert (new Card(4, 'h'), new Card(3, 's')) ==
false.
 *
 * @covers Card::isInMatchingSet
 */
public function testIsInMatchingSet2()
```

```
    {
        $this->assertFalse(
            $this->object->isInMatchingSet(new Card(4, 'h'), new Card(3,
 's'))
        );
    }
```

You'll notice that for each `@assert` annotation, a corresponding test method was created.

Using the Skeleton Generator for test-driven development

The Skeleton Generator can also be used when employing a test-driven development methodology. The examples so far have been focused on creating tests based on written code. This is contradictory to the test-driven development methodology. However, you can create code from tests just as easily as you can create tests from code. When you run `phpunit-skelgen --class - CardTest test/CardTest.php` from the project directory you will see that it creates a new `Card` class in `src/Card.php`. It even stubs the methods that it detects based on the test methods you wrote.

```php
<?php
/**
 * Generated by PHPUnit_SkeletonGenerator 1.2.0 on 2013-02-11 at
00:12:00.
 */
class Card
{
    /**
     * @todo Implement getNumber().
     */
    public function getNumber()
    {
        // Remove the following line when you implement this method.
        throw new RuntimeException('Not yet implemented.');
    }

    /**
     * @todo Implement getSuit().
     */
    public function getSuit()
    {
        // Remove the following line when you implement this method.
        throw new RuntimeException('Not yet implemented.');
    }

    /**
     * @todo Implement isInMatchingSet().
```

```
        */
        public function isInMatchingSet()
        {
            // Remove the following line when you implement this method.
            throw new RuntimeException('Not yet implemented.');
        }
}
```

Using test fixtures (Simple)

As you begin writing tests you'll find that many of them, especially ones inside the same test case class, need to run the same code to set up the object that you are running tests against. This code is part of what is commonly called a fixture. Many test methods require the same fixture. PHPUnit allows you to support shared fixtures using the `setUp()` and `tearDown()` methods.

You have undoubtedly seen these methods implemented in some of our examples already. We will now go into further detail of how these fixtures work and what types of things you can do with them.

How to do it...

Open `tests/CardTest.php` and add a new `setUp()` method and use the `$card` property to hold the `Card` fixture.

```php
<?php
class CardTest extends PHPUnit_Framework_TestCase
{
    private $card;
    public function setUp()
    {
        $this->card = new Card('4', 'spades');
    }
    public function testGetNumber()
    {
        $actualNumber = $this->card->getNumber();
        $this->assertEquals(4, $actualNumber, 'Number should be <4>');
    }
    public function testGetSuit()
    {
        $actualSuit = $this->card->getSuit();
        $this->assertEquals('spades', $actualSuit, 'Suit should be
<spades>');
    }
```

```
public function testIsInMatchingSet()
{
  $matchingCard = new Card('4', 'hearts');
  $this->assertTrue($this->card->isInMatchingSet($matchingCard),
      '<4 of Spades> should match <4 of Hearts>');
}
public function testIsNotInMatchingSet()
{
  $matchingCard = new Card('5', 'hearts');
  $this->assertFalse($this->card->isInMatchingSet($matchingCard),
      '<4 of Spades> should not match <5 of Hearts>');
}
}
```

How it works...

You'll notice the biggest change in this method is the addition of the setUp() method. The setUp() method is run immediately before any test method in the test case. So when testGetNumber() is run, the PHPUnit framework will first execute setUp() on the same object. setUp() then initializes $this|card with a new Card object. $this|card is then used in the test to validate that the number is returned properly. Using setUp() in this way makes your tests much easier to maintain. If the signature of the Card class's constructor is changed, you will only have one place in this file to reflect that change as opposed to four separate places. You will save even more time as you add more and more tests to a single test case class.

It should also be noted that a new instance of CardTest is created each time a test method is executed. Only the code in this case is being shared. The objects that setUp() creates are not shared across tests. We will talk about how to share resources across tests shortly.

There is also a tearDown() method. It can be used to remove any resource you created inside your setUp() method. If you find yourself opening files, or sockets, or setting up other resources then you will need to use tearDown() to close those resources, delete file contents, or otherwise tear down your resources. This becomes very important to help keep your test suite from consuming too many resources. There is nothing quite like running out of inodes when you are running a large test suite!

There's more...

As we mentioned a moment ago, PHPUnit has the facility to share resources across execution of multiple tests. This is generally considered bad practice. One of the primary rules of creating tests is that tests should be independent from each other so that you can isolate and locate the code causing test failures more easily.

However, there are times when the physical resources required to create a fixture become large enough to outweigh the negatives of sharing this fixture across multiple tests. When such cases arise PHPUnit provides two methods that you can override: setUpBeforeClass() and tearDownAfterClass(). These are expected to be static methods. setUpBeforeClass() will be called prior to any tests or setUp() calls being made on a given class. tearDownAfterClass() will be called once all tests have been run and the final tearDown() call has been made. If you override these methods to create new objects or resources you would need to make sure that you set these values on static members of the test case class. Also, even if you are dealing only with objects, the tearDownAfterClass() is incredibly important to implement. If you do not implement it then any object created in setUpBeforeClass() and saved to static variables will remain in memory until all tests in your test suite have run.

Using data providers (Intermediate)

Data providers are a great way to test many different variants of a single method call quickly. When you have a method that is responsible for applying an algorithm to the method arguments and come up with a predictable result then data providers are a great option.

How to do it...

Modify the contents of test/CardTest.php to the following:

```php
<?php
class CardTest extends PHPUnit_Framework_TestCase
{
  private $card;
  public function setUp()
  {
    $this->card = new Card('4', 'spades');
  }
  public function testGetNumber()
  {
    $actualNumber = $this->card->getNumber();
    $this->assertEquals(4, $actualNumber, 'Number should be <4>');
  }
  public function testGetSuit()
  {
    $actualSuit = $this->card->getSuit();
    $this->assertEquals('spades', $actualSuit, 'Suit should be
<spades>');
  }
  public function matchingCardDataProvider()
  {
```

```
      return array(
        array(new Card('4', 'hearts'), true, 'should match'),
        array(new Card('5', 'hearts'), false, 'should not match')
      );
    }

    /**
     * @dataProvider matchingCardDataProvider
     */
    public function testIsInMatchingSet(Card $matchingCard, $expected,
$msg)
    {
        $this->assertEquals($expected, $this->card->isInMatchingSet($matc
hingCard),
            "<{$this->card->getNumber()} of {$this->card->getSuit()}>
{$msg} "
            . "<{$matchingCard->getNumber()} of {$matchingCard-
>getSuit()}>");
    }
}
```

How it works...

The new `matchingCardDataProvider()` method is our data provider. It should return an array containing multiple arrays of arguments to pass into a test method. The method does need to be public as it actually gets called from outside the test case. Also, the method does not have to be static, as you do not have reliable access to any variable you should treat the method as though it were static.

You then need to assign the data provider to one of your test methods. This is done using the `@dataProvider` annotation. In this example, the annotation is assigned to the `testIsInMatchingSet()` method. You will notice that this method has three parameters. This is exactly the same number of items there are in each sub-array returned by `matchingCardDataProvider()`.

The three parameters in this example are the arguments provided for `isInMatchingSet()`, an expected value, as well as part of the assertion failure message. When using data providers you can use the **Don't Repeat Yourself** (**DRY**) principal very effectively to reduce the amount of code you have to write for each test. However, this does need to be balanced with readability. If you reduce the amount of code that has to be written, but someone else can't understand what the test is doing then the effectiveness and maintainability of the test is actually reduced.

Identifying test failures

You may be wondering how to identify which data set failed while using the data providers. Fortunately, PHPUnit takes care of this for you. Modify the `matchingCardDataProvider()` method to return a row that will force the test to fail.

```php
public function matchingCardDataProvider()
{
  return array(
    array(new Card('4', 'hearts'), true, 'should match'),
    array(new Card('5', 'hearts'), false, 'should not match'),
    array(new Card('4', 'clubs'), false, 'should not match')
  );
}
```

Then, run the unit test suite and you will see the following:

```
environment — vagrant@precise64: /book — ssh — 99×20

vagrant@precise64:/book$ phpunit
PHPUnit 3.7.10 by Sebastian Bergmann.

Configuration read from /book/phpunit.xml

....F

Time: 0 seconds, Memory: 2.75Mb

There was 1 failure:

1) CardTest::testIsInMatchingSet with data set #2 (Card, false, 'should not match')
<4 of spades> should not match <4 of clubs>
Failed asserting that true matches expected false.

/book/test/CardTest.php:35

FAILURES!
Tests: 5, Assertions: 5, Failures: 1.
vagrant@precise64:/book$
```

As you can see it tells you the index of the data set along with the actual parameters passed as a part of that data set.

This can be improved even further by providing keys to the array that your data provider returns. Try using the following data provider:

```php
public function matchingCardDataProvider()
{
  return array(
    '4 of Hearts' => array(new Card('4', 'hearts'), true, 'should
match'),
    '5 of Hearts' => array(new Card('5', 'hearts'), false, 'should not
```

```
match'),
        '4 of Clubs' => array(new Card('4', 'clubs'), false, 'should not
match')
    );
}
```

Run the tests again to see the following output:

As you can see, you can utilize data providers to not only consolidate your code, but you can also make it very easy to isolate the data set you have problems with.

Using test dependencies (Advanced)

When you begin writing tests for one of your classes you may notice that when one aspect of functionality for your class breaks, many tests fail. Quite often a method of a class will have some preconditions that must be true for it to behave properly in a given situation. A classic example of this is a stack. If you cannot construct a stack properly then any further tests against that stack are most likely going to fail.

You can use PHPUnit's test dependency feature to help with this. When you indicate that one test is dependent on another test, PHPUnit will skip the dependent test whenever its dependencies do not successfully pass. Test dependencies also allow you to enable producer-consumer relationships into your test suites. One test case will "produce" the input for another test case to "consume".

We will take a look at how test dependencies can work by writing a test for our CardCollection class that looks at how cards are added to the deck.

How to do it...

Place the following code to the `test/CardCollection.php` file:

```php
<?php
class CardCollectionTest extends PHPUnit_Framework_TestCase
{
  private $cardCollection;

  public function setUp()
  {
    $this->cardCollection = new CardCollection();
  }

  public function testCountOnEmpty()
  {
    $this->assertEquals(0, $this->cardCollection->count());
  }

  /**
   * @depends testCountOnEmpty
   */
  public function testAddCard()
  {
    $this->cardCollection->addCard(new Card('A', 'Spades'));
    $this->cardCollection->addCard(new Card('2', 'Spades'));

    $this->assertEquals(2, $this->cardCollection->count());

    return $this->cardCollection;
  }

  /**
   * @depends testAddCard
   */
  public function testGetTopCard(CardCollection $cardCollection)
  {
    $card = $cardCollection->getTopCard();

    $this->assertEquals(new Card('2', 'Spades'), $card);
  }
}
```

How it works...

In your new file you have two test methods using a @depends annotation. This is the annotation that enables PHPUnit's test dependency functionality. This annotation, essentially, tells PHPUnit that you do not want to run the following test unless the test referenced in the @depends annotation has passed. If this test has not passed then the following test will be skipped. If for some reason the CardCollection::count() method was not running properly and caused the testCountOnEmpty() test to fail then testAddCard() would be skipped. This can be easily seen by breaking the testCountOnEmpty() test on purpose by inserting $this|fail('testing @depends') in the test and rerunning your tests.

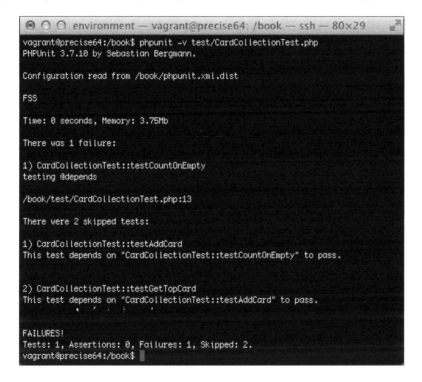

```
● ○ ○   environment — vagrant@precise64: /book — ssh — 80×29
vagrant@precise64:/book$ phpunit -v test/CardCollectionTest.php
PHPUnit 3.7.10 by Sebastian Bergmann.

Configuration read from /book/phpunit.xml.dist

FSS

Time: 0 seconds, Memory: 3.75Mb

There was 1 failure:

1) CardCollectionTest::testCountOnEmpty
testing @depends

/book/test/CardCollectionTest.php:13

There were 2 skipped tests:

1) CardCollectionTest::testAddCard
This test depends on "CardCollectionTest::testCountOnEmpty" to pass.

2) CardCollectionTest::testGetTopCard
This test depends on "CardCollectionTest::testAddCard" to pass.


FAILURES!
Tests: 1, Assertions: 0, Failures: 1, Skipped: 2.
vagrant@precise64:/book$
```

Another interesting aspect of the @depends annotation is the producer-consumer aspect of it. Whenever you mark a test with the @depends annotation the return value from the test specified in the annotation will be provided as the argument to the test being annotated. This is what is happening in the testGetTopCard() method. The testAddCard() method returns the card collection being tested. This value then persists for any test that depends on this method. As soon as we annotated testGetTopCard() with @depends testGetTopCard, PHPUnit is triggered to pass the populated card collection as the first parameter.

This does a couple things for you. It doesn't bother to try and pull the top card if it appears that addCard() is not working. It also prevents you from having to repeat the code necessary to populate your card collection.

Another thing to note is that the @depends annotations always reference a test above the annotation. The @depends annotation never influences the order of tests. Tests will always be run from the top of the file to the bottom of the file. If the @depends annotation references a method below the annotation it will simply skip the test as the dependency has not yet passed.

Multiple test dependencies

You can add multiple @depends annotations to a single test. PHPUnit will then check to ensure that all of the tests specified have passed before running a given test. If the dependencies also return values, they will all be accessible as arguments in the order they are specified. The following code shows how this works:

```php
<?php
class DependencyTest extends PHPUnit_Framework_TestCase
{

    public function test1()
    {
        $this->assertTrue(true);
        return 1;
    }

    public function test2()
    {
        $this->assertTrue(true);
        return 2;
    }

    public function test3()
    {
        $this->assertTrue(true);
        return 3;
    }

    /**
     * @depends test1
     * @depends test2
     * @depends test3
     */
    public function testDependencies($arg1, $arg2, $arg3)
    {
        $this->assertEquals(1, $arg1);
        $this->assertEquals(2, $arg2);
        $this->assertEquals(3, $arg3);
    }
}
```

Multiple dependent tests

You can also have the same test referenced by @depends multiple times. You do need to be very careful when doing this. Copies are not made of any objects returned. So if you modify the object in any way in the first dependent test, those modifications will also be present in the second dependent test. This can be seen in the following code:

```php
<?php
class DependencyTest extends PHPUnit_Framework_TestCase
{

    public function testCreateStdClass()
    {
        $obj = new stdClass();
        $obj->foo = 'bar';
        $this->assertTrue(true);
        return $obj;
    }

    /**
     * @depends testCreateStdClass
     */
    public function testDependency1($obj)
    {
        $this->assertEquals('bar', $obj->foo);
        $obj->foo = 'notbar';
    }

    /**
     * @depends testCreateStdClass
     */
    public function testDependency2($obj)
    {
        $this->assertEquals('notbar', $obj->foo);
    }
}
```

Using mock objects (Simple)

When writing unit tests you should always strive to isolate the code that you are testing as much as possible. This can be difficult at times. It is very common for methods in a class to interact with other classes. This interaction means that executing the method you are testing will result in you not only testing that method but you will also, in a sense, be testing all of the methods on external objects that this method calls. Ideally, you would only want to test the interaction with these methods. You would not want the testing to reach into the external method itself. To help solve this problem the concept of a mock object was created.

Mock objects are lightweight implementations or extensions of interfaces and objects that implement the public interface in a controlled way. When creating a mock object you can specify that any of that object's public or protected methods return a specific value. You can also set expectations as to how a method of that object will be called. This allows you to keep your tests focused on the specific class or method you want to test.

PHPUnit has an entire mocking library built directly into the framework. In recent years, some alternative mocking libraries such as Phake and Mockery have also been created.

How to do it...

Create the following test case in `test/PlayerTest.php`:

```php
<?php
class PlayerTest extends PHPUnit_Framework_TestCase
{
  private $player;
  private $hand;

  public function setUp()
  {
    $this->hand = $this->getMock('CardCollection');
    $this->player = new Player('John Smith', $this->hand);
  }

  public function testDrawCard()
  {
    $deck = $this->getMock('CardCollection');
    $deck->expects($this->once())
        ->method('moveTopCardTo')
        ->with($this->identicalTo($this->hand));

    $this->player->drawCard($deck);
  }

  public function testTakeCardFromPlayer()
  {
```

```
    $otherHand = $this->getMock('CardCollection');
    $otherPlayer = $this->getMock('Player', array(), array('Jane
Smith', $otherHand));
    $card = $this->getMock('Card', array(), array('A', 'Spades'));

    $otherPlayer->expects($this->once())
        ->method('getCard')
        ->with($this->equalTo(4))
        ->will($this->returnValue($card));

    $otherPlayer->expects($this->once())
        ->method('getHand')
        ->will($this->returnValue($otherHand));

    $this->hand->expects($this->once())
        ->method('addCard')
        ->with($this->identicalTo($card));

    $otherHand->expects($this->once())
        ->method('removeCard')
        ->with($this->identicalTo($card));

    $this->assertTrue($this->player->takeCards($otherPlayer, 4));
    }
}
```

How it works...

The getMock() method is used to create a mock. The first parameter passed to this method is the name of the class or interface you are mocking. This method will inspect the class or interface you pass to it and will either extend it (if it is a class) or implement it (if it is an interface.) If no other parameters are given, any method that is not declared as private, final, or static will be overridden to simply return null. You can also pass an array of methods in the mocked class that you wish to override. This allows for creating partial mocks.

A couple of the `getMock()` calls in the example also pass an array of values as the third parameter. These values are used to construct the mock object. When mock objects for classes are created, the original constructor of that class is called by default. If you do not pass the parameters you would like to use to the constructor, you will get an error similar to the one shown as follows:

```
● ○ ○   environment — vagrant@precise64: /book — ssh — 80×21
vagrant@precise64:/book$ phpunit test/PlayerTest.php
PHPUnit 3.7.10 by Sebastian Bergmann.

Configuration read from /book/phpunit.xml

.E

Time: 0 seconds, Memory: 3.00Mb

There was 1 error:

1) PlayerTest::testTakeCardFromPlayer
Missing argument 1 for Card::__construct(), called in /usr/share/php/PHPUnit/Fra
mework/MockObject/Generator.php on line 237 and defined

/book/src/Card.php:24
/book/test/PlayerTest.php:27

FAILURES!
Tests: 2, Assertions: 1, Errors: 1.
vagrant@precise64:/book$ ▮
```

If your tests do not need to utilize the values in the constructor then you can prevent the mock object from calling the original constructor. This can be accomplished by setting the fifth parameter of `getMock()` to `false`.

The `testTakeCardFromPlayer()` method in the preceding example could be modified to create its mocks as shown next and the test will continue to run with no problem. You should prevent constructor calls whenever possible.

```php
public function testTakeCardFromPlayer()
{
    $otherHand = $this->getMock('CardCollection');
    $otherPlayer = $this->getMock('Player', array(), array(), '',
false);
    $card = $this->getMock('Card', array(), array(), '', false);

    // Continue method...
}
```

You may be wondering now what that fourth parameter is for. The fourth parameter of getMock() allows you to specify the name for the new mock class. This is not something that is typically necessary. If you need to skip the constructor and do not want to create a custom name for the new mock class you can simply pass an empty string.

Once the mock is created you will typically need to either stub a method or create expectations for methods on that mock. In testDrawCard() we just needed to ensure that the moveTopCardTo() method was being called with the appropriate arguments. If you want to set an expectation such as this you call the expects() method on your mock. The expects() method takes an invocation matcher as its argument. The best way to think about invocation matchers is as a counter of when or how often a method should be called. The PHPUnit_Framework_TestCase class has several methods that can be passed to expects() such as any(), never(), atLeastOnce(), once(), exactly(), and at(). All of these methods with the exception of at() are used to indicate the number of times you are expecting the method being mocked to be a call. So if you specify once() then the method you are calling can only be called once. If it is not called or is called multiple times then your expectation will not be met and your test will generate a failure similar to the following screenshot:

```
environment — vagrant@precise64: /book — ssh — 80×21

vagrant@precise64:/book$ phpunit test/PlayerTest.php
PHPUnit 3.7.10 by Sebastian Bergmann.

Configuration read from /book/phpunit.xml

F.

Time: 0 seconds, Memory: 3.25Mb

There was 1 failure:

1) PlayerTest::testDrawCard
CardCollection::moveTopCardTo(Mock_CardCollection_a7f0d4c4 Object (...)) was not
  expected to be called more than once.

/book/src/Player.php:24
/book/test/PlayerTest.php:20

FAILURES!
Tests: 2, Assertions: 4, Failures: 1.
vagrant@precise64:/book$
```

Once you have set your expectation you must specify the method you are setting the expectation on. This is done by calling the method() method on the result of expects(). The only parameter of this method is the name of your mock object's method that you want to set expectations on.

The final step in defining an expectation on a mock is to set the expected parameters. This is done by calling the `with()` method. You can see the `with()` method being called with a single argument in the `testDrawCard()` method. You will pass as many arguments to `with()` as you would see passed to the method you are mocking. By default PHPUnit will attempt to verify that the argument passed to `with()` is equal to the argument passed to the mocked method. You can also use any of PHPUnit's constraints to check for other aspects of each argument. For instance, in `testTakeCardFromPlayer()` you will see that the `identicalTo()` method is being used so we can validate the exact instance of an object. Any assertions that are defined in PHPUnit will also have a constraint counterpart that can be used when mocking objects.

If you want to control the return value for the method that you are mocking you can use the `will()` method in addition to the `with()` method. The `will()` method takes a single parameter that allows you to specify what will be returned from the method. This is done using one of PHPUnit's stub methods. The most common method and the one that is used in the example is `returnValue()`. This allows you to specify the specific value that the method should return.

There's more...

Mock objects can be used for much more than simple stubbing and verifications. Now that you are aware of the basics we can discuss some other common uses of mock objects. You can find thorough documentation on PHPUnit's mock object functionality at `http://phpunit.de/manual/current/en/test-doubles.html`.

Thoughts on partial mocks

You should avoid partial mocks whenever possible. They tend to contribute to hard-to-maintain tests as you will often find yourself having to adjust the methods being mocked. A common use of partial mocks is to prevent a protected method from executing in the class you are testing. This usually indicates that you have one class doing too much. That protected method would likely be better served as a method in a separate class that you can then create a full mock for. Another use for partial mocks is to mock abstract classes. This is actually a fairly good use of partial mocks; however, there is a better way to handle this that will keep your tests easy to maintain. We will discuss this later.

Ignoring parameters on method expectations

Occasionally, you won't really care about what or how many parameters were used to call a method. When this is the case you can use the `withAnyParameters()` method instead of `with()`. This will essentially match any call to the given method.

Stubbing exceptions

When you find yourself writing tests for exception handling, you will find it necessary to stub a method to throw an exception. This can be done using PHPUnit's `throwException()` method. This is very useful in helping to make sure you are handling exceptions in third-party code (or even your own code) gracefully. It takes an instantiated exception as its only argument.

```php
public function testThrowException()
{
  $card = $this->getMock('Card', array(), array(), '', false);

  $card->expects($this->any())
      ->method('getNumber')
      ->will($this->throwException(new RuntimeException('Test
Exception')));

  // verify that the exception above is thrown.
  $this->setExpectedException('RuntimeException', 'Test Exception');
  $card->getNumber();
}
```

Stubbing multiple return values

Occasionally, you will need a method to return one of many values. There are a few ways this can be handled. The first way is with a return value map. A return value map specifies a list of arrays that contains a value for every parameter passed to the mocked method and an additional value at the end for the return value. If a set of parameters do not exist in the map then null is returned. You will notice we are using the `any()` matcher as we know the method is going to be called multiple times.

```php
public function testReturnValueMap()
{
  $calculator = $this->getMock('TestCalculator');

  $valueMap = array(
    array(1, 2, 3),
    array(2, 4, 6),
    array(1, 4, 5)
  );

  $calculator->expects($this->any())
      ->method('add')
      ->will($this->returnValueMap($valueMap));

  // Test Return Values
  $this->assertEquals(3, $calculator->add(1, 2));
```

```
        $this->assertEquals(6, $calculator->add(2, 4));
        $this->assertEquals(5, $calculator->add(1, 4));
        $this->assertNull($calculator->add(1,3));
    }
```

If the order of a specific set of calls is well defined, then you can use the onConsecutiveCalls() method. This method accepts any number of arguments and will return each one in order for every call made to the mocked method. If you do not have as many arguments as there are method calls, then it will begin returning null after there are no more arguments left to return.

This is a very effective way to test code utilizing an iterator-like interface. For instance, given code such as the following:

```
    while (!$this->game->isOver())
    {
      // ...
    }
```

You can guarantee that the loop is executed twice using the following mock definition:

```
    $mock->expects($this->any())
        ->method('isOver')
        ->will($this->onConsecutiveCalls(false, false, true));
```

Stubbing with callbacks

Perhaps the most flexible thing you can do when creating a stub is using a callback. This allows you to define an anonymous function to generate a return value. While this can get complicated, it does give you the ability to simplify tests if you use it wisely.

If the addCard() method was responsible for returning the current size of the collection after the card was added, and we tested a method that relied on that behavior, one way we could implement it is using a callback.

```
    public function testReturnCallback()
    {
      $deck = $this->getMock('CardCollection');

      $deck->expects($this->any())
          ->method('addCard')
          ->will($this->returnCallback(function (Card $card) {
            static $collectionSize = 0;
            $collectionSize++;
            return $collectionSize;
          }));
```

```
// Test Return Values
$this->assertEquals(1, $deck->addCard(new Card('A', 'Hearts')));
$this->assertEquals(2, $deck->addCard(new Card('2', 'Hearts')));
$this->assertEquals(3, $deck->addCard(new Card('3', 'Hearts')));
}
```

Using mock builders

In our examples so far we have used PHPUnit's original mock functionality. PHPUnit 3.5 introduced a concept called `MockBuilder`. The purpose of `MockBuilder` is to clean up the instantiation of mock objects. As we have already discussed, the parameters of `getMock()` can get very confusing. You can use the mock builder to try and make your tests more readable. Each of the various arguments we specified for `getMock()` are represented by separate methods on the builder. For instance, the ability to disable the constructor can instead be enabled by calling `disableOriginalConstructor()` on your builder. An example of how `testTakeCardFromPlayer()` could benefit from this feature when creating mocks can be seen as follows:

```
public function testTakeCardFromPlayer()
{
  $otherHand = $this->getMock('CardCollection');
  $otherPlayer = $this->getMockBuilder('Player')
      ->disableOriginalConstructor()
      ->getMock();
  $card = $this->getMockBuilder('Card')
      ->disableOriginalConstructor()
      ->getMock();
  // ...
}
```

Using alternative mock frameworks

While PHPUnit's mock framework provides a significant amount of functionality there are other libraries that can be used in conjunction with PHPUnit that provide a more robust feature set. In many cases, despite this robustness, the libraries are also easier to use.

Phake

Phake is an alternative mocking framework to PHPUnit's built-in mocking framework. The primary motive behind its creation was to present an alternative to the concept of expectations that PHPUnit utilizes. It, instead, treats mock object expectations as assertions that you execute after your test code has run, utilizing Phake's verification framework. An example of how `PlayerTest` can be rewritten using Phake is shown as follows:

```
<?php
class PhakePlayerTest extends PHPUnit_Framework_TestCase
{
```

```
    private $player;

    /**
     * @Mock CardCollection
     */
    private $hand;

    public function setUp()
    {
      Phake::initAnnotations($this);
      $this->player = new Player('John Smith', $this->hand);
    }

    public function testDrawCard()
    {
      $deck = Phake::mock('CardCollection');
      $this->player->drawCard($deck);
      Phake::verify($deck)
          ->moveTopCardTo($this->identicalTo($this->hand));
    }

    public function testTakeCardFromPlayer()
    {
      $otherHand = Phake::mock('CardCollection');
      $otherPlayer = Phake::mock('Player');
      $card = Phake::mock('Card');

      Phake::when($otherPlayer)
          ->getCard(Phake::anyParameters())->thenReturn($card);
      Phake::when($otherPlayer)
          ->getHand()->thenReturn($otherHand);

      $this->assertTrue($this->player->takeCards($otherPlayer, 4));

      Phake::verify($this->hand)
          ->addCard($this->identicalTo($card));
      Phake::verify($otherHand)
          ->removeCard($this->identicalTo($card));
    }
  }
}
```

An exhaustive discussion of Phake is outside the scope of this book. However, you can learn more about Phake at `https://github.com/mlively/Phake`.

Mockery

Another alternative mock object framework is Mockery. It is similar in concept to PHPUnit's own mock framework but makes some adjustments to its API to make what is being done by the code more clear to the readers. An example of `PlayerTest` written with Mockery is shown as follows:

```php
<?php
class MockeryPlayerTest extends PHPUnit_Framework_TestCase
{
  private $player;
  private $hand;

  public function setUp()
  {
    $this->hand = \Mockery::mock('CardCollection');
    $this->player = new Player('John Smith', $this->hand);
  }

  public function testDrawCard()
  {
    $deck = \Mockery::mock('CardCollection');
    $deck->shouldRecieve('moveTopCardTo')
        ->with($this->identicalTo($this->hand));

    $this->player->drawCard($deck);
  }

  public function testTakeCardFromPlayer()
  {
    $otherHand = \Mockery::mock('CardCollection');
    $otherPlayer = \Mockery::mock('Player');
    $card = \Mockery::mock('Card');

    $otherPlayer->shouldReceive('getCard')
        ->with(4)
        ->andReturn($card);

    $otherPlayer->shouldReceive('getHand')
        ->andReturn($otherHand);

    $this->hand->shouldReceive('addCard')
        ->with($this->identicalTo($card));

    $otherHand->shouldReceive('removeCard')
```

```
                    ->with($this->identicalTo($card));

         $this->assertTrue($this->player->takeCards($otherPlayer, 4));
     }
}
```

For more information about Mockery see `https://github.com/padraic/mockery`.

Testing abstract classes (Intermediate)

When we were discussing mock objects the concept of partial mocks was introduced. One common use of partial mocks is to test abstract classes. Abstract classes can't be tested directly as by definition they cannot be instantiated. You can always create an extension of the abstract class just for testing. However, PHPUnit provides functionality to very easily mock abstract classes so that only the abstract methods get mocked. All other functions will execute normally.

How to do it...

In `src/Player.php` is a `Player` class shown as follows:

```php
<?php
abstract class Player
{
  // ...

  public function requestCard()
  {
    $cardNumber = $this->chooseCardNumber();

    if (!$this->hasCard($cardNumber))
    {
      throw new RuntimeException('Invalid card chosen by player');
    }

    return $cardNumber;
  }

  abstract protected function chooseCardNumber();

  // ...
}
```

The corresponding test can be placed in `test/PlayerTest.php` to test the abstract nature of the class.

```php
<?php
class PlayerTest extends PHPUnit_Framework_TestCase
{
private $player;
  private $hand;

  public function setUp()
  {
    $this->hand = new CardCollection();
    $this->hand->addCard(new Card('A', 'Spades'));
    $this->player = $this->getMockForAbstractClass('Player',
array('John Smith', $this->hand));
  }

  public function testRequestCardCallsChooseCardNumber()
  {
    $this->player->expects($this->once())
      ->method('chooseCardNumber')
      ->will($this->returnValue('A'));

    $this->assertEquals('A', $this->player->requestCard());
  }
}
```

How it works...

The PHPUnit method `getMockForAbstractClass()` can be used to generate a partial mock where only the abstract methods of a given class are overridden. The argument list for `getMockForAbstractClass()` is similar to the argument list for `getMock()`. The big difference is that the list of methods to mock is moved from being the second parameter to being the last parameter. By default `getMockForAbstractClass()` will mock only the abstract methods of the class. If you find yourself needing to override this functionality then you should just use `getMock()` instead.

In this example, the `Player` class is being mocked with a player name and a `CardCollection` object is being passed to the `Player` instance's constructor. The `testRequestCardCallsChooseCardNumber()` method is assuring that the `Player::chooseCardNumber()` method is called as a part of `Player::requestCard()` and is then ensuring that the value returned by `chooseCardNumber()` is subsequently returned by `requestCard()`.

You could use `getMock()` for this instead. The `setUp()` method could be rewritten to use `getMock()` to set up the partial mock.

```php
public function setUp()
{
  $this->hand = new CardCollection();
  $this->hand->addCard(new Card('A', 'Spades'));
  $this->player = $this->getMock('Player', array('chooseCardNumber'),
array('John Smith', $this->hand));
}
```

The advantage of using `getMockForAbstractClass()` is that you do not have to add to the mocked method list (the second parameter of `getMock()`) every time you add a new abstract method to the class. It also keeps the test significantly more concise.

Abstract classes in Phake

Phake also provides a function that assists in testing abstract classes.
`Phake::partialMock()` works in a similar fashion to the PHPUnit counterpart.

```php
<?php
class PhakePlayerTest extends PHPUnit_Framework_TestCase
{
private $player;
  private $hand;

  public function setUp()
  {
    $this->hand = new CardCollection();
    $this->hand->addCard(new Card('A', 'Spades'));
    $this->player = Phake::partialMock('Player', 'John Smith', $this-
>hand);
  }

  public function testRequestCardCallsChooseCardNumber()
  {
    Phake::when($this->player)->chooseCardNumber()->thenReturn('A');

    $this->assertEquals('A', $this->player->requestCard());

    Phake::verify($this->player)->chooseCardNumber();
  }
}
```

The `Phake::partialMock()` method accepts the class name as the first parameter. The remaining parameters will be used in the constructor of the mock object. This method works in mostly the same way as `getMockForAbstractClass()`. It creates a mock that will call the original method for any non-abstract method.

Testing traits (Intermediate)

Traits are a new concept introduced in PHP 5.4. Similar to Abstract classes they cannot be instantiated directly. You can always create a test class that uses a particular trait to test the functionality in that trait. However, PHPUnit has built-in functionality to dynamically create classes that use traits. This allows for simple testing of traits.

How to do it...

Consider a modified version of the `CardCollection` class that is, instead, represented as a trait.

```php
<?php

trait CardCollectionTrait
{
  //...
  public function count()
  {
    return count($this->cards);
  }
  //...
}
```

You can create a test similar to what was created earlier for the `CardCollection` class.

```php
<?php
class CardCollectionTraitTest extends PHPUnit_Framework_TestCase
{
  private $cardCollection;

  public function setUp()
  {
    $this->cardCollection = $this->getObjectForTrait('CardCollectionTrait');
  }

  public function testCountOnEmpty()
  {
```

```
    $this->assertEquals(0, $this->cardCollection->count());
  }
  //...
}
```

How it works...

Similar to how PHPUnit can be used to generate concrete implementations of abstract classes, it can also be used to generate a user of a given trait. The `PHPUnit_Framework_TestCase::getObjectForTrait()` method will generate and instantiate a class that uses the trait you pass as the first argument. You can then test the trait as you would test any other class.

Testing exceptions and errors (Intermediate)

A negative test is a test that is created to show error conditions or exceptions from the system under test. Negative tests can be easy to ignore. However, it is not only important to make sure your code works the way it is supposed to but it is also important to know that it also fails the way it is supposed to.

Fortunately, PHPUnit provides very easy to use functionality to help ensure that your code is throwing errors and exceptions at the appropriate time.

How to do it...

This functionality can be shown through some negative tests for the following code:

```php
<?php
abstract class Player
{
  // ...

  public function requestCard()
  {
    $cardNumber = $this->chooseCardNumber();

    if (!$this->hasCard($cardNumber))
    {
      throw new RuntimeException('Invalid card chosen by player');
    }

    return $cardNumber;
```

```
    }

    // ...
  }
```

To properly test that the exception is being thrown we can write the following test:

```php
<?php
class PlayerTest extends PHPUnit_Framework_TestCase
{
  public function testRequestCardThrowsOnInvalidCard()
  {
    $this->player->expects($this->once())
        ->method('chooseCardNumber')
        ->will($this->returnValue('2'));

    $this->setExpectedException('RuntimeException', 'Invalid card
chosen by player');
    $this->player->requestCard();
  }
}
```

How it works...

You can test that your code throws an exception using the setExpectedException()
method. This tells PHPUnit to make sure that a specified exception is thrown before the test is
finished. It takes the fully qualified class name of the exception as the first parameter. You can
specify an optional second and third parameter with the expected message and code for the
exception. If either of these parameters are not specified then the message and code will not
be checked.

In this test, you are setting up the player class to choose a card number that does not
currently exist in the hand. When this occurs a RuntimeException should be thrown
with the message **Invalid card chosen by player** when Player::requestCard()
is called. In the event that the error doesn't get thrown the test will fail.

There's more...

PHPUnit also allows you to specify expected exceptions using annotations.

```
/**
 * @expectedException RuntimeException
 * @expectedExceptionMessage Invalid card chosen by player
 */
public function testRequestCardThrowsOnInvalidCardUsingAnnotation()
```

```
{
    $this->player->expects($this->once())
        ->method('chooseCardNumber')
        ->will($this->returnValue('2'));

    $this->player->requestCard();
}
```

Instead of using the `setExpectedException()` method you can use the `@expectedException` annotation. The `@expectedException` annotation accepts the fully qualified class name of the exception that should be thrown. The `@expectedExceptionMessage` annotation accepts the message that should be set on the exception. There is also an `@expectedExceptionCode` annotation that can be used to set an exception code if necessary.

Testing output (Intermediate)

While PHP started out as a web-based scripting language, over the years it has become more and more common for command line scripts to be created as well. One of the common pieces of functionality for these scripts is the output of text to the command line. While one could make the argument that testing the output falls outside of the realm of unit testing, it does not fall outside of the realm of PHPUnit's functionality.

PHPUnit makes it very simple to capture and validate text that has been output to the command line.

How to do it...

The following code echoes text to the command line.

```php
<?php
class CliFormatter
{
    // ...
    public function announcePlayerHand(Player $player)
    {
        echo "Current Hand: ", $this->getCards($player->getHand()),
"\n\n";
    }
    // ...
}
```

This code can be tested to ensure it outputs what you would expect with the following code below:

```php
<?php
class CliFormatterTest extends PHPUnit_Framework_TestCase
{
  private $formatter;

  public function setUp()
  {
    $this->formatter = new CliFormatter();
  }

  public function testAnnouncePlayerHand()
  {
    $cards = new CardCollection();
    $cards->addCard(new Card('A', 'Spades'));
    $cards->addCard(new Card('2', 'Spades'));

    $player = $this->getMock('HumanPlayer', array(), array(), '',
false);
    $player->expects($this->once())
      ->method('getHand')
      ->will($this->returnValue($cards));

    $this->expectOutputString("Current Hand: AS 2S \n\n");
    $this->formatter->announcePlayerHand($player);
  }
}
```

How it works...

The expectOutputString() method can be used to determine if your code is outputting what you expect to the command line. PHPUnit uses PHP's output buffering functionality to capture anything that is sent to the script's stdout command. The expectOutputString() method will compare the string you pass to it to the buffer at the end of the test. If the values do not match, PHPUnit will fail that test.

You can also match the output with a regular expression using expectedOutputRegex(). We could rewrite the expectedOutputString() call as follows:

```php
$this->expectOutputRegex('/^Current Hand: AS 2S\s+$/');
```

This is a convenient way to help get rid of the sensitivity to white spaces that `expectedOutputString()` has. A better way to handle a white space in your output is to use `setOutputCallback()`. This method can be used to manipulate the output before it is checked against the expectations set by `expectedOutputRegex()` or `expectedOutputString()`. One of these manipulations could be to trim all whitespace:

```
public function testAnnouncePlayerHandCallback()
{
    $cards = new CardCollection();
    $cards->addCard(new Card('A', 'Spades'));
    $cards->addCard(new Card('2', 'Spades'));

    $player = $this->getMock('HumanPlayer', array(), array(), '',
false);
    $player->expects($this->once())
        ->method('getHand')
        ->will($this->returnValue($cards));

    $this->expectOutputString("Current Hand: AS 2S");
    $this->setOutputCallback(function ($output) {
        return trim($output);
    });
    $this->formatter->announcePlayerHand($player);
}
```

There's more...

When PHPUnit is running in the strict mode it will emit an error whenever the test writes an output to the screen. To prevent this from happening you simply need to turn off the strict mode in the XML configuration and discontinue the use of the `--strict` command line flag when running the test suite.

Testing protected and private methods (Intermediate)

A common question of those that are getting started with unit testing is, how are protected and private methods tested? Protected and private methods are not uncommon and the desire to test the code in them should be natural. The confusion that arises from how to test these methods is created at least in part by the thought that they must be tested independently.

In the book *Pragmatic Unit Testing*, *Dave Thomas* and *Andy Hunt* had this to say:

> *In general, you don't want to break any encapsulation for the sake of testing (or as mom used to say, "don't expose your privates!"). Most of the time, you should be able to test a class by exercising its public methods. If there is significant functionality that is hidden behind private or protected access, that might be a warning sign that there's another class in there struggling to get out.*

Using the public interface of your class is by far the best way to test protected and private methods. If you find yourself unable to do this, PHPUnit and PHP itself offer solutions to test these methods directly.

How to do it...

The following code in the `CardCollection` class is used to add a card to the collection:

```php
<?php
class CardCollection implements IteratorAggregate
{
  // ...
  public function addCard(Card $card)
  {
    array_push($this->cards, $card);
  }
  // ...
}
```

The following test can be used to ensure the object state is modified accordingly:

```php
<?php
class CardCollectionTest extends PHPUnit_Framework_TestCase
{
  // ...
  public function testAddCardAffectAttribute()
  {
    $card = new Card('A', 'Spades');
    $this->cardCollection->addCard($card);
    $this->assertAttributeEquals(array($card), 'cards', $this-
>cardCollection);
  }
  // ...
}
```

How it works...

This test shows how you can inspect the private or protected state of a given object. PHPUnit has a series of attribute assertions that you can use to test the value of any attribute on a class even if it has protected or private visibility. Whenever possible you should use the public interface of an object to test this; however, in the event that it is not possible, the attribute assertions can come in very handy. The `assertAttributeEquals()` method is similar to its non-attribute counterpart `assertEquals()`. However, instead of passing the value you are testing, you pass the name of the attribute you want to test as the second parameter and the object that attribute is set on as the third parameter. As always, the expected value is passed in as the first parameter.

PHPUnit contains attribute equivalents for the standard set of assertions. You can compare values, check contents of arrays, compare array counts, and so on. Anything you would typically do with a variable in a unit test can also be accomplished in attributes using the attribute assertions.

Private and protected methods

PHPUnit doesn't provide the same functionality above for private and protected methods. However, if you are using PHP 5.3.2 or higher you can use reflection to alter the visibility of the method you are trying to test.

In `CliFormatter` there is a private method, `getCard()`, that is used to format a given card into a readable string.

```php
<?php
class CliFormatter
{
  // ...
  private function getCard(Card $card)
  {
    return $card->getNumber() . substr($card->getSuit(), 0, 1);
  }
  // ...
}
```

Using reflection we can expose this method and invoke it as a part of a test.

```php
<?php
class CliFormatterTest extends PHPUnit_Framework_TestCase
{
  // ...
  public function testGetCard()
  {
    $method = new ReflectionMethod('CliFormatter', 'getCard');
    $method->setAccessible(true);
```

```
    $card = new Card('A', 'Spades');
    $this->assertEquals('AS', $method->invoke($this->formatter,
$card));
  }
  // ...
}
```

The `ReflectionMethod::setAccessible()` method can be used to allow a method to be invoked. However, you must invoke that method using the `ReflectionMethod::invoke()` method. If we attempted to call `$this|formatter|getCard()` directly then it would fail. This does keep us from having to clean up the accessibility. Your client code will continue to work as you originally wrote it. You don't have to worry about the method continuing to be accessible.

Testing database interaction (Advanced)

A large part of many applications written in PHP revolve around database interaction. While it largely falls outside the realm of the official definition of unit testing, testing database interaction is very important. If the integration between the code of your application and the database that stores your application's data is important then it should be tested. This is another case where you can use PHPUnit to do more than simple unit tests.

There are a few different options for testing database interaction with PHPUnit. PHPUnit has an extension that you can load that is based on the Java DBUnit library. There is also a newer package called Machinist that takes a different but, in most cases, a much simpler approach to database testing. You can find out more information on Machinist at `https://github.com/stephans/phpmachinist`.

Database testing is centered on making sure that you are inserting, deleting, and updating data in your database properly and making sure your application is pulling the appropriate data out of the database. You are able to test cases where you are modifying the database by comparing the contents of a database to an expected result set. You are able to test queries against the database by comparing the output of various queries to an expected result set. You will often need to have data in the database at the beginning of your test for this functionality to work properly.

Getting ready

The database extension for PHPUnit comes as a separate PEAR package. In order to run the tests in the following examples you will need to install this extension. You can do so with the following command:

```
sudo pear install pear.phpunit.de/DbUnit
```

The examples will be based on a SQLite install. So, make sure you have the SQLite extension and client installed. The method of installing this depends on your operating system and distribution. The examples in this recipe are going to be based on the following schema definition:

```
CREATE TABLE game (
  id INTEGER PRIMARY KEY AUTOINCREMENT,
  date_created DATETIME,
  current_player_id INTEGER
);

CREATE TABLE player (
  id INTEGER PRIMARY KEY AUTOINCREMENT,
  game_id INTEGER,
  name VARCHAR,
  hand VARCHAR
);
```

The schema will be loaded into the `data/game-test.db` file.

How to do it...

1. Place the following code in `src/SqliteManager.php`.

```php
<?php
class SqliteManager {
  private $sqliteConnection;

  public function __construct(PDO $sqliteConnection)
  {
    $this->sqliteConnection = $sqliteConnection;
  }

  public function updateGame($gameId, $currentPlayerName)
  {
    $gameUpdateQuery = "
      UPDATE game
      SET current_player_id = (
        SELECT id
        FROM player
        WHERE
          game_id = ?
          AND name = ?
        )
      WHERE id = ?
```

```
    ";

    $stm = $this->sqliteConnection->prepare($gameUpdateQuery);
    $stm->execute(array($gameId, $currentPlayerName, $gameId));
  }
  // ...
}
```

2. Update your configuration in `phpunit.xml.dist` to include the highlighted line.

```
<phpunit
    bootstrap="test-bootstrap.php"
    colors="false"
    strict="true"
>
  <!-- other content -->
  <php>
    <includePath>src</includePath>
    <const name="DB_DSN" value="sqlite:data/game-test.db" />
  </php>
  <!-- other content -->
</phpunit>
```

3. Create the following file in `test/BaseDatabaseTest.php`.

```
<?php

abstract class BaseDatabaseTest extends PHPUnit_Extensions_
Database_TestCase
{
  protected static $testPdo;

  protected static $systemPdo;

  public static function setUpBeforeClass()
  {
    self::$testPdo = new PDO(DB_DSN);
    self::$testPdo->setAttribute(PDO::ATTR_ERRMODE, PDO::ERRMODE_
EXCEPTION);
    self::$systemPdo = new PDO(DB_DSN);
    self::$systemPdo->setAttribute(PDO::ATTR_ERRMODE,
PDO::ERRMODE_EXCEPTION);
  }

  public static function tearDownAfterClass()
  {
    self::$testPdo = null;
```

```
      self::$systemPdo = null;
    }

    protected function getConnection()
    {
      return $this->createDefaultDBConnection(self::$testPdo);
    }
  }
```

4. Create your PHPUnit test in `test/SqliteManagerTest.php`.

```php
<?php
class SqliteManagerTest extends BaseDatabaseTest
{
  private $sqliteManager;

  public function setUp()
  {
    parent::setUp();

    $this->sqliteManager = new SqliteManager(self::$systemPdo);
  }

  /**
   * @group db
   */
  public function testUpdateGame()
  {
    $this->sqliteManager->updateGame(1, 'Player2');

    $expectedDataSet = $this->createXMLDataSet(__DIR__ . '/
expected/SqliteManagerTestUpdateGame.xml');
    $this->assertDataSetsEqual($expectedDataSet, $this-
>getConnection()->createDataSet(array('game')));
  }

  // More tests …

  protected function getDataSet()
  {
    return $this->createXMLDataSet(__DIR__ . '/fixtures/
SqliteManagerTest.xml');
  }
}
```

5. Create an XML data set fixture in `test/fixtures/SqliteManagerTest.xml`.

```xml
<?xml version="1.0" ?>
<dataset>
  <table name="game">
    <column>id</column>
    <column>date_created</column>
    <column>current_player_id</column>
    <row>
      <value>1</value>
      <value>2013-03-01 00:00:00</value>
      <value>1</value>
    </row>
  </table>
  <table name="player">
    <column>id</column>
    <column>game_id</column>
    <column>name</column>
    <column>hand</column>
    <row>
      <value>1</value>
      <value>1</value>
      <value>Player1</value>
      <value>A Hearts,2 Clubs,3 Diamonds,4 Spades,5 Hearts</value>
    </row>
    <row>
      <value>2</value>
      <value>1</value>
      <value>Player2</value>
      <value>6 Hearts,7 Clubs,8 Diamonds,9 Spades,10 Hearts</value>
    </row>
  </table>
</dataset>
```

6. Create an XML data set expectation in `test/expected/SqliteManagerTestUpdateGame.xml`.

```xml
<?xml version="1.0" ?>
<dataset>
  <table name="game">
    <column>id</column>
    <column>date_created</column>
    <column>current_player_id</column>
    <row>
      <value>1</value>
```

```
        <value>2013-03-01 00:00:00</value>
        <value>2</value>
      </row>
    </table>
  </dataset>
```

How it works...

There are a lot of moving parts involved with database testing. You have to set up your connection to the database, create the fixtures for the database, and create the expected data that you will compare the database against. There are many ways that these steps can be done. The preceding files show how this can be done for almost any scenario.

The first change that you need to make is to allow the database that you are using to be configurable. This isn't absolutely necessary, but it will make future changes significantly easier should you ever decide to alter your data source. Earlier we discussed PHPUnit configuration and discovered the power you have in the `phpunit.xml` file. One of the items in the PHP environment that can be configured from here are PHP constants.

Here we used the `<const />` element to define the `DB_DSN` constant to point to our test SQLite database. Constants are a great way to configure test cases. They are easy to access from within the test and they can be very simple to override when using the `phpunit.xml.dist` model. You just redefine them in a new `phpunit.xml` file or in an alternate `config` file.

Once you have defined your connection information you should create a base database test case that sets up your connections for you. This will provide a place for the global database test configuration. This class should be used for any kind of convenience method to help you reduce code duplication in your tests. For this example, we are just using this class to set up our database connections. There were two database PDO connections defined: `BaseDatabaseTest::$testPdo` and `BaseDatabaseTest::$systemPdo`. You don't have to define two different connections for tests. However, it is recommended that you do so to isolate the database used by the system under testing from the database used to run the test. This helps to ensure that you aren't polluting any kind of connection-based data such as the result of MySQL's `LAST_INSERT_ID()` function. This can also be very important when testing transactions. If you have code that uses transactions to ensure data integrity but it does not properly commit the transaction and you use the same connection to load the data for assertions that was used in the actual test, everything will pass just fine. In that case, it is not until you use a separate testing connection that cannot see unclosed transactions that you will realize the data was never committed.

It is important to note that the `setUpBeforeClass()` method was used to set up the connections. This can save a significant amount of time as the database connection will only need to be established once per database test case class as opposed to once per method. This does not strictly adhere to the principal of isolating your tests from each other as much as possible, but the speed benefit of reusing a connection almost always outweighs the isolation benefit. If `setUpBeforeClass()` is used to establish your database connections, you must use `tearDownAfterClass()`. This is necessary because the PDO connections are being assigned to class statics. These will never fall out of scope by themselves, which is necessary for PDO connections to close. To ensure this does not happen, the `tearDownAfterClass()` method is used to set the connections to null.

Once the PDO connections are established the `getConnection()` method is used to wrap your PDO connection into DBUnit's connection format. The value returned from `getConnection()` will be used to set up your data fixtures as well as to pull data to validate again at the end of your tests.

With the `BaseDatabaseTest` test case, each of our test cases can be specifically focused on the unique system targeted for testing. In this example, the system being tested is the `SqliteManager` class. Each test case that focuses on database interaction will require a small amount of data to be present in the database at the beginning of each test. The `getDataSet()` method can be used to identify this initial data set, which will be populated in your database at the beginning of each test.

There are several formats that can be used to define the data set. Each of these formats has a method in `PHPUnit_Extensions_Database_TestCase` to allow you to easily instantiate the data set. In this example, `createXMLDataSet()` is used. It takes a path to an XML file as its only parameter. It is good practice to keep these files all in a single directory relative to the PHPUnit test case class. This makes it very easy to understand which files go with which tests without having to look at code. You can see the `SqliteManagerTestUpdateGame.xml` being loaded as our data set fixture.

The `SqliteManagerTestUpdateGame.xml` file uses the standard XML format for PHPUnit's database extension. The structure of this format is pretty simple. The root element `<dataset>` will contain one or more `<table>` elements. The `<table>` element has a `name` attribute that defines the name of the table. It will then have one or more `<column>` elements that will define the columns in each table. Finally, there will be one or more `<row>` elements each containing a number of `<value>` elements equal to the number of columns defined for that table. To define a null value in any one of the columns you can instead use an empty `<null />` element.

A very common mistake in creating database tests happens when the `setUp()` method is overwritten. In this test case, it was overwritten to instantiate the `SqliteManager` class. It is important to ensure the parent is called whenever this method is overwritten. If `parent::setUp()` method is not called, then your initial data set will never be loaded. Unfortunately, there is not a great indication in the test that this is what happened.

Now is a good time to go through the life cycle of a database test. When a database test is run, at the time that `setUp()` is run, `getConnection()` is called. The connection returned is then used to delete all data in the tables specified by the `getDataSet()` method. Then the data set itself is reinserted. At that point the individual test is run. Finally, the tear down methods are invoked. So in this example, during `setUp()` the tables defined in the data set are game and player. Both of these tables will be completely deleted. Then the three rows specified in the data set will be inserted. Then the test itself will be run. The test in `testUpdateGame()` is very simple. It just invokes the `SqliteManager::updateGame()` method and then validates the content in the database.

When testing functionality that updates your data you will need to validate the resultant data in the database. To establish your expected data set you can use `createXMLDataSet()` just like you used it in `getDataSet()`. You will be passing in a different data set than what was used in `getDataSet()`. In this example, the `SqliteManagerTestUpdateGame.xml` data set was used. If part of your test is to ensure that nothing in your data was changed you can just as easily re-use the data set returned by `getDataSet()`. To keep your data sets organized, I would recommend you keep your fixture data sets separate from your expected data sets. One exception of course is those cases where you re-use your fixture as your expectation. This will help you keep your test cases organized as your suite grows.

The `assertDataSetsEqual()` can be used to compare the actual data in your database with the expected data set. Your expected data set should be passed as the first parameter. The actual data set can be retrieved directly from the connection returned by `getConnection()`. The connection object has a `createDataSet()` method that will create a data set containing all of the rows in all of the tables in the database. You can narrow the data set down to the tables that you are concerned with by specifying an array of table names as the first argument to `createDataSet()`.

When one of your database tests fail, PHPUnit does its best to format the failure in an easily readable format. If we broke the previous test by failing to execute the update query, the test would fail as shown in the following screenshot:

The table containing the differences will be printed out with the data contained. If there are multiple tables involved you will see the differences in all of the tables. This can be a lot of information if there are large data sets involved. This is one really good reason to keep the size of your data sets as small as possible for expectations.

There's more...

Only the surface of database testing has been scratched with this example. There are many other functions and features available to help make this testing easier for you. We will cover a few of the these functions now but I would encourage you to take a look at PHPUnit's online database testing chapter to get more details about database testing: `http://www.phpunit.de/manual/3.7/en/database.html`.

Alternate data sets

You have seen how you can use PHPUnit's XML format to define your data set; however, there are several other data set formats that you will find useful.

Flat XML data set

There are several other data set formats that can be used for your fixtures other than the standard XML format. You can also use a simpler (though less flexible) flat XML format where a single element defines a single row. The name of each element corresponds to the name of the table the row will be inserted in and the attribute names correspond to column names. The `SqliteManagerTest.xml` file could be rewritten using the flat format shown as follows:

```xml
<?xml version="1.0" ?>
<dataset>
  <game
      id="1"
      date_created="2013-03-01 00:00:00"
      current_player_id="1"
      />
  <player
      id="1"
      game_id="1"
      name="Player1"
      hand="A Hearts,2 Clubs,3 Diamonds,4 Spades,5 Hearts"
      />
  <player
      id="2"
      game_id="1"
      name="Player2"
      hand="6 Hearts,7 Clubs,8 Diamonds,9 Spades,10 Hearts"
      />
</dataset>
```

This format is much more concise but you lose the flexibility to specify things such as null values. If you want to use this format, instead of using the `createXMLDataSet()` method you can use `createFlatXMLDataSet()`.

MySQL XML data set

The MySQL XML data set can be very useful if you are using the MySQL database engine. This data set type allows you to use `mysqldump` to generate data sets. The key is using the `--xml` argument for `mysqldump`.

```
mysqldump --xml -t -u [username] --password=[password] [database] > /
path/to/file.xml
```

You can then pass the path of the resultant file to the `createMySQLXMLDataSet()` method to convert this file to a PHPUnit data set.

```
$this->createMySQLXMLDataSet('/path/to/file.xml');
```

YAML data set

The last data set we will talk about here is the YAML data set. This can provide a nice compromise of the conciseness of the flat XML data set with the flexibility of the standard XML data set. The `SqliteManagerTest.xml` data set can be redefined as a YAML data set as follows:

```
game:
    -
    id: 1
    date_created: "2013-03-01 00:00:00"
    current_player_id: 1

player:
    -
    id: 1
    game_id: 1
    name: Player1
    hand: A Hearts,2 Clubs,3 Diamonds,4 Spades,5 Hearts
    -
    id: 2
    game_id: 1
    name: Player2
    hand: 6 Hearts,7 Clubs,8 Diamonds,9 Spades,10 Hearts
```

The convenience of this format over the flat XML format is that you can specify a null by simply excluding the value just as you would in a typical YAML file. The unfortunate part of YAML is that there is no convenience method to create a data set in this format. You must instantiate it directly.

```
protected function getDataSet()
{
  return new PHPUnit_Extensions_Database_DataSet_YamlDataSet(
      __DIR__ . '/fixtures/SqliteManagerTestYaml.yaml'
  );
}
```

Validating your data with queries

Sometimes it can be somewhat tedious to create expected data sets for full tables. For instance, you may have a lot of columns that aren't germane to the application but are just used for book keeping such as creation time or modified time types of columns. If you would like to assert against a portion of your data, a great strategy can be to use a query to generate the actual data set.

The database connection object returned by `getConnection()` has a `createQueryTable()` method that can be used to create a table object based on the result of a select query. When using this method to validate the results of your table you will have to use the `assertTablesEqual()` method instead of `assertDataSetsEqual()`. The `createQueryTable()` method takes two parameters. The first parameter is the name you want to use for the table. This name should match the name of the table in your expected data set. The second parameter is the query to populate the table.

The `testUpdateGame()` method could be rewritten to take advantage of query tables.

```
public function testUpdateGame()
{
  $this->sqliteManager->updateGame(1, 'Player2');

  $expectedDataSet = $this->createXMLDataSet(__DIR__ . '/expected/
SqliteManagerTestUpdateGame.xml');
  $actualTable = $this->getConnection()->createQueryTable("game",
"SELECT * FROM game");
  $this->assertTablesEqual($expectedDataSet->getTable('game'),
$actualTable);
}
```

Viewing code coverage (Advanced)

We have gone over a lot of PHPUnit functionality and how to use this functionality to build a test suite. Once you have a test suite created it is good to understand how effective your unit tests are. One way you can measure the effectiveness of your tests is by seeing how much of your code is actually under test. This is commonly referred to as your test suite's code coverage. PHPUnit has very useful reporting tools to help measure and monitor this coverage.

Getting ready

To generate code coverage reports you must have XDebug installed. This can typically be accomplished using your operating system's packaging system.

How to do it...

Make the following modifications to the `phpunit.xml.dist` file as shown by the highlighted lines of code:

```
<phpunit
    bootstrap="test-bootstrap.php"
    colors="false"
    strict="true"
>
  <!-- other content -->
  <logging>
    <log type="coverage-html" target="build/html-coverage"
charset="UTF-8" highlight="true" />
  </logging>
  <filter>
    <whitelist processUncoveredFilesFromWhitelist="true">
      <directory suffix=".php">src</directory>
    </whitelist>
  </filter>
</phpunit>
```

Now any test runs will also generate an HTML code coverage report for your code.

How it works...

There are a couple of new PHPUnit configuration options presented here. The first and more important one is done via the `<logging>` and child `<log>` element. We are instructing PHPUnit to use the coverage-HTML logger type. You must specify a `target` attribute. This can be either a relative or absolute path to a directory that the HTML will be written to. If the directory does not already exist, it will be created. You can also specify the `charset` attribute that should be used to generate the HTML as well as whether or not the PHP source code will have syntax highlighting.

The second configuration you can use is the `<filter>` element. This is used to specify a white list, a black list, or both of files that you want to be included in your code coverage report. Generally, you should use a white list with the `processUncoveredFilesFromWhitelist` attribute set to `true`. This will make sure that all files in that directory are included in the coverage report. Otherwise, only files that are actually loaded will be added to the report. This means you run the risk of files that have 0 percent coverage falling off of the coverage report completely. This will give you a false confidence in the coverage of your tests.

The contents of your white list should be the code for the system you are testing. Usually, there is not much value to your testing to be gained by including the third-party code or the test code itself. These filters can be used to ensure this third party and test code is not considered in your coverage reports.

The `<whitelist>` element can include one or more of the `<directory>` and `<file>` elements. These elements contain absolute or relative paths to the directory or file that should be included. The `<directory>` element also accepts a suffix attribute to further filter the contents by the contained files' suffix. In our case, we used `.php`. In addition to these two elements, you can also include an `<exclude>` element. This element also takes one or more `<directory>` or `<file>` elements. This can be used if there are specific files or directories that are in white listed directories but should be excluded. It should be noted that you can use wildcards (`*`) in any of these elements.

If for some reason you would prefer to use a black list, then you simply need to use the `<blacklist>` element instead. There are no attributes for `<blacklist>` and you would use the same child elements as you would use with `<whitelist>`.

Now, when the `phpunit` command is run, an HTML version of the coverage report will be written to `book/build/html-coverage/index.html`.

This displays all of the files in our `src` directory along with a summary of the test coverage in that file. There are three different types of code coverage that are broken down for the directory as a whole as well as each individual file.

The line coverage is the first measurement. It is a percentage of the executable lines of code that are executed by the test suite. The function or method coverage is the percentage of methods or functions in the file/directory that have full code coverage. Full code coverage means that every executable line in the method or function has been executed at least once. The final metric, classes and traits coverage, is the percentage of classes or traits in a file or directory that have full code coverage.

From this view you can drill into your directories. This would show a view similar to what you've already seen. If you click on a file however, you start seeing some very useful information.

This view presents a summary of the coverage of a specific file. It will include a count of the classes in the file as well as how many of those classes have full coverage. It will then break down each method or function in the file and report whether or not that function has full coverage, and how many lines in each method is covered.

Each method also gives a **Change Risk Anti-Patterns** (**CRAP**) index. CRAP is a good metric for identifying methods that are hesitant to change. It is a function that ascertains the complexity of a method and the amount of coverage the method currently has. All other things equal, the more complex a method the higher is its CRAP index. The index is lowered as you create more tests that cover more of a method.

There is no hard-and-fast method for determining the optimal CRAP index. So I will leave the details for that debate to other books and papers. I prefer to see methods with CRAP indexes less than 10.

Once you get below the summary table you will see a syntax highlighted rendering of the source code for the file. Each executable line will be highlighted either in red or green. If it is red, that means it is not covered by any tests in your suite. If it is green, that means the line is covered by one or more tests. If you hover over a green line, it will show a list of all the tests that cover that specific line. You may occasionally see lines highlighted yellow. These are dead lines. This means that due to the structure of the code, the yellow highlighted line could never possibly be executed. This is usually because of a return statement somewhere other than the end of your method or function.

PHPUnit also provides a dashboard view of your project at `book/build/html-coverage/index.dashboard.html`.

This dashboard provides four interesting pieces of information. The class coverage distribution shows you how many classes in the system fall within a specified range of code coverage. In an ideal project only the right-most bar would have any size. That would mean that all of your classes have full code coverage. This project is problematic as you can see that a large number of classes have absolutely no coverage.

The second section is a scatter plot of the class complexity. The Y-axis measures complexity and the X-axis measures code coverage. The ideal code has lots of coverage and little complexity, so the ideal location for your plots is going to be in the lower-right corner of this graph. The worst possible location for any plot is the upper-left corner. If you see a plot in that area, you can find the class that is the culprit by hovering over the plot.

The third section shows your top project risks. This gives you a more comprehensible view of what you see in the class complexity chart. You can use it to identify where your testing effort should be focused. The classes here are determined by using the CRAP index we already covered.

The final section is the least tested methods section. This gives you an overview of the methods with the least amount of testing focus. This drills down even further on areas that can be improved in your test cases.

There is a wealth of information that can be a great help in improving an existing test suite's coverage. It can also go great lengths in keeping the quality of an already good test suite high.

About Packt Publishing

Packt, pronounced 'packed', published its first book "*Mastering phpMyAdmin for Effective MySQL Management*" in April 2004 and subsequently continued to specialize in publishing highly focused books on specific technologies and solutions.

Our books and publications share the experiences of your fellow IT professionals in adapting and customizing today's systems, applications, and frameworks. Our solution based books give you the knowledge and power to customize the software and technologies you're using to get the job done. Packt books are more specific and less general than the IT books you have seen in the past. Our unique business model allows us to bring you more focused information, giving you more of what you need to know, and less of what you don't.

Packt is a modern, yet unique publishing company, which focuses on producing quality, cutting-edge books for communities of developers, administrators, and newbies alike. For more information, please visit our website: www.packtpub.com.

Writing for Packt

We welcome all inquiries from people who are interested in authoring. Book proposals should be sent to author@packtpub.com. If your book idea is still at an early stage and you would like to discuss it first before writing a formal book proposal, contact us; one of our commissioning editors will get in touch with you.

We're not just looking for published authors; if you have strong technical skills but no writing experience, our experienced editors can help you develop a writing career, or simply get some additional reward for your expertise.

Expert PHP 5 Tools

ISBN: 978-1-84719-838-9   Paperback: 468 pages

Proven enterprise development tools and best practices for designing, coding, testing, and deploying PHP applications

1. Best practices for designing, coding, testing, and deploying PHP applications – all the information in one book

2. Learn to write unit tests and practice test-driven development from an expert

3. Set up a professional development environment with integrated debugging capabilities

JavaScript Unit Testing

ISBN: 978-1-78216-062-5   Paperback: 190 pages

Your comprehensive and practical guide to efficiently performing and automating JavaScript testing

1. Learn and understand, using practical examples, synchronous and asynchronous JavaScript unit testing

2. Cover the most popular JavaScript Unit Testing Frameworks including Jasmine, YUITest, QUnit, and JsTestDriver

3. Automate and integrate your JavaScript Unit Testing for ease and efficiency

Please check **www.PacktPub.com** for information on our titles

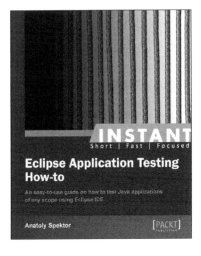

Instant Eclipse Application Testing How-to

ISBN: 978-1-78216-324-4   Paperback: 62 pages

An easy-to-use guide on how to test Java applications of any scope using Eclipse IDE

1. Learn something new in an Instant! A short, fast, focused guide delivering immediate results

2. Learn how to install Eclipse and Java for any platform

3. Get to grips with how to efficiently navigate in the Eclipse environment using shortcuts

4. Create your own Java sample app and learn how to test and debug it using a rich set of Eclipse debugging tools

Using Node.js for UI Testing

ISBN: 978-1-78216-052-6   Paperback: 146 pages

Learn how to easily automate testing of your web apps using Node.js, Zombie.js and Mocha

1. Use automated tests to keep your web app rock solid and bug-free while you code

2. Use a headless browser to quickly test your web application every time you make a small change to it

3. Use Mocha to describe and test the capabilities of your web app

Please check **www.PacktPub.com** for information on our titles

Printed in Great Britain
by Amazon